THE VOICE OF VOICES

THE VOICE OF VOICES

NORTH MIAMI SENIOR HIGH
HOME OF THE PIONEERS

Written by Dr. Judith Grey's Poetry Club of 2022/2023

THE VOICE OF VOICES
From the Students at North Miami Senior High
Home of the Pioneers
Written by Dr. Judith Grey's Poetry Club of 2022/2023

Copyright © 2023 by GoPublish

All rights reserved.

This is a work of fiction. Names, characters, places and incidents either are the product of the authors' imagination or are used fictitiously, and any resemblance to any actual persons, living or dead, events, or locales is entirely coincidental.

No part of this book may be reproduced or transmitted in any form or by any means, electronic or mechanical, including photocopying, recording, or by any information storage and retrieval system, without permission in writing from the copyright owner.

Published by GoPublish, a division of Visual Adjectives.
Delray Beach, Florida.
WWW.VISUALADJECTIVES.COM
INFO@VISADJ.COM

ISBN-13: 978-1-941901-47-2 trade paperback
ISBN-10: 1-941901-47-6 trade paperback

First American Paperback Edition: May 2023

CONTENTS

7 | FOREWORD
BY DR. JUDITH GREY

9 | ADMINISTRATIVE STAFF

10 - 11 | DR. JUDITH GREY'S
POETRY CLUB OF 2022/2023

12 | CHAPTER ONE
DREAMS
BY NAHIDA NELSON

14 | CHAPTER TWO
LOVE IS DANGEROUS
BY COLMISE JEAN-BAPTISTE

16 | CHAPTER THREE
A PLACE WHERE LOVE DIES
BY CHRISTNYCK GAY

18 | CHAPTER FOUR
I FORGIVE YOU
BY SACHA ROMULUS

20 | CHAPTER FIVE
NATURE
BY CARL B. CHARLES

22 | CHAPTER SIX
PERFECT PEACE
BY DIANE FABIEN

24 | CHAPTER SEVEN
HER IMAGINATION
BY ESTHERLANDE VIGILE

26 | CHAPTER EIGHT
THERE'S THIS PERSON
BY KINBERLIE JOSEPH

28 | CHAPTER NINE
RESPECTING OTHERS
BY ALLEY BAZILE

30 | CHAPTER TEN
HEALED ME
BY VENISSA LOUISSAINT

32 | CHAPTER ELEVEN
SELF WORTH AND SELF-LOVE
BY GARDINA JEAN-BAPTISTE

36 | CHAPTER TWELVE
HIGH
BY CIARRA MORESTAN

38 | CHAPTER THIRTEEN
THUNDERSTORM
BY SARA JUSTE

40 | CHAPTER FOURTEEN
DARK SKIN GIRLS
BY MARLANDE ALLIANCE MAËLLE

44 | CHAPTER FIFTEEN
TRUTH
BY THED-FANA PRINCE

46 | CHAPTER SIXTEEN
I AM
BY GALLY DUCASSE

48 | CHAPTER SEVENTEEN
I AM
BY KETNAYDINE EDOUARD

50 | CHAPTER EIGHTEEN
BEAUTY
BY SANAA ROBERTSON

52 | CHAPTER NINETEEN
TRUE WARRIOR
BY RICHARD PAUL

54 | CHAPTER TWENTY
DREAMS
BY AXEL GOMEZ-MONTEPEQ

56 | CHAPTER TWENTY-ONE
LOVE
BY KETNAYDINE EDWARD

58 | CHAPTER TWENTY-TWO
7 BILLION PATHS
BY MEDEFCA METELLUS

60 | CHAPTER TWENTY-THREE
LIFE
BY GALLY DUCASSE

62 | CHAPTER TWENTY-FOUR
WOMEN EMPOWERMENT
BY MARLINA SOUFFRANTT

64 | CHAPTER TWENTY-FIVE
WHO AM I
BY MEILLEUR FLORELEA

66 | CHAPTER TWENTY-SIX
WHERE I'M FROM
BY ALIYA BAPTISTE

68 | CHAPTER TWENTY-SEVEN
NEEDS OF THE WORLD
BY DANIEL GONZALEZ

72 | CHAPTER TWENTY-EIGHT
FAMILY KINDNESS AND LOVE
BY FREDERICK HYPPOLITE

74 | CHAPTER TWENTY-NINE
YOUR LOVE
BY EMELY ACOSTA

76 | CHAPTER THIRTY
BARON DOCTOR
BY CHRIST THOMAS

78 | CHAPTER THIRTY-ONE
I AM ALIYA
BY ALIYA BAPTISTE

80 | CHAPTER THIRTY-TWO
MY FLYING ANGEL
BY MORESHA GUILLAUME

82 | CHAPTER THIRTY-THREE
LIFE WITHOUT MOTHER
BY PATRIANNA REYNA ASTIN

84 | CHAPTER THIRTY-FOUR
MY DAY
BY OLIVIER COTIERE

86 | CHAPTER THIRTY-FIVE
OPEN WATERS
BY ELIJAH JOSEPH

88 | CHAPTER THIRTY-SIX
DELUSIONAL POEM
BY NACHCA PIERRE

90 | CHAPTER THIRTY-SEVEN
JOURNEY TO HOME
BY UNIKA PIERRE

92 | CHAPTER THIRTY-EIGHT
LIKE A PHOENIX I RISE FROM THE ASHES
BY KAYTORA PAUL

94 | CHAPTER THIRTY-NINE
THE PLAYBOY
BY CHARVENS SAINTEUS

96 | CHAPTER FORTY
VARIATIONS ON DREAMS
BY FERLENS FREDERIC

98 | CHAPTER FORTY-ONE
A POEM TO MY MOM
BY LEISSA PUTHIOT

100 | CHAPTER FORTY-TWO
I ONCE SAID
BY CARLA LOUIS

102 | CHAPTER FORTY-THREE
FREE
BY DENNIS BROWN-FIGUEROA

104 | CHAPTER FORTY-FOUR
LOVE
BY BARBARA AUGUSTE

106 | CHAPTER FORTY-FIVE
HAPPINESS
BY CURTIS DORCELY

108 | CHAPTER FORTY-SIX
LOVE'S BEAUTY POEM
BY DOROTHY LODZ-CHAMMA PIERRE

110 | CHAPTER FORTY-SEVEN
ABROAD
BY UNIKA PIERRE

A MIND UNOCCUPIED
IS A MIND WASTED.

FOREWORD

My students are amazing. It's such a joy to educate them despite the nuances that comes with teaching. After all, they are just like students anywhere in the world. These students tend to speak what is on their minds, harbor similar thoughts, crave for the same things, and share their experiences relentlessly. Whether in English, Spanish, French, or Haitian Creole, when given the task to write individually in a corner of the classroom, under a tree, on a bench outside, or in the living area in their homes, amazingly, their thoughts conveyed universal teenage conclusions. This is not based on assumptions, but facts untainted in their voices.

This year, the students at the North Miami Senior High School poetry club decided to share their expressions publicly. The idea is to tell their story in their own way, shape, and form. Under my leadership and guidance, students were allowed to express themselves freely on whatever topic or issue interest them in poetry. Hence, they projected their voices. The authors of this book are ninth through twelfth grade students who are members of 'Broken Pieces' the poetry club.

Students raising their voices strengthen their relationship with each other and create a sense of belonging. These students took the initiative to be proactive and express their thoughts wholeheartedly. Some conveyed successes, some failures, some determination, some love but through it all resilience. It's important for students to be empowered through their voices. They need to be supported especially when they are crying out for help. Students need to affect change one way or another. Yes, their opinions and thoughts matter. We beg of you not to be judgmental but to be understanding of the creative young minds.

DR. JUDITH GREY

ADMINISTRATIVE STAFF

North Miami Senior High
Home of the Pioneers

Miriame Stewart | Principal

Elvira Ruiz-Carrillo | Vice Principal

Enock Alouidor | Assistant Principal

Lashawn Gaskin | Assistant Principal

Mimose Morgan-Rose | Assistant Principal

North Miami Senior High
Home of the Pioneers
Dr. Judith Grey's Poetry Club of 2022/2023

CHAPTER ONE
DREAMS
by Nahida Nelson

THE VOICE OF VOICES

You should hold on to your dreams.
For dreams are meant to come true.
Life is like a rollercoaster.
You will always have good and bad days.
Life is like a barren field frozen with ice and snow.
You are a beautiful human being,
who got goals and dreams set for yourself.
Your uniqueness is what brought you into this world.
You have many talents to share
with the beautiful people in this world.
Your story will captivate many young men and women's hearts.
Use it to not only help others but to inspire them.
Be surrounded by positive people who truly knows your potential.
Life is a blessing.
Love yourself for the person you are!

CHAPTER TWO
LOVE IS DANGEROUS
by Colmise Jean-Baptiste

THE VOICE OF VOICES

Love, love is beautiful
Like the stars in the sky at night,
Shine like a big diamond in the sunlight,
And sweet like an apple pie.

But love, love can make you insane,
And make the blood in your veins stop circulating
Like a plane getting carried away by the confused signals received,
And can make you believe that it can make you live the happiest days.

Ignoring the red flags and falling in love
With an unknown at first sight,
May mentally lead you to a maze with no escape,
That is when you try to take a deep breath,
But feel too suffocated.

With the thoughts of being trapped
In a world of depression
And to be in your bubble of desperation to be loved.
Till you conclude that
LOVE IS DANGER.

CHAPTER THREE
A PLACE WHERE LOVE DIES
by Christnyck Gay

THE VOICE OF VOICES

Love, my love is dead
A place where happiness should be filled
Was a place where darkness takes presence.

Love, memories that love creates
Turned into an unknown moment of becoming strangers.
A moment of being lonely with love still in my heart.

Even if our love is dead, in my heart, you will always be present
In my head it's you, every heartbeat is your laughter,
but why bother?
The day you turned away, the day we became strangers,
the day you pretended to not see me....
Did you ever see me? Was I ever visible to you?

You used to be something like a beautiful daisy,
now you're like a rose, with your thorns, you hurt me.
As beautiful and tender, as stubborn, and selfish.
Your happiness makes me sadder,
knowing our chapter in the book was erased.
Never write your story in PEN you'll erase later,
not everyone stays a lover and no love lasts forever.

Dr. Judith Grey's Poetry Club of 2022/2023

CHAPTER FOUR
I FORGIVE YOU
by Sacha Romulus

THE VOICE OF VOICES

I forgive you, after all forgiveness is the key to kindness.
I forgive you for all your mistakes and blames.
I forgive you for not always being there.
I forgive you for all the broken promises,
I know all your mistakes are haunting you,
but you'll find your way back, and it will be too late.
However, there will never be a chance again, that's no debate.
Forgiveness is the key to kindness.
What does a clueless and mannerless person like you know about forgiveness and kindness?
Let's emphasize, you are uncivilized.
Slowly, day by day, you become more and more barbarous.
Like all your broken promises that have forgotten who owned them.
I will forgive for the things you put me through
I will forgive for all the fake smiles and promises
I will forgive for all of the things you said to me
I will forgive for all of the people you got involved
I will not forgive for how you made me feel.

CHAPTER FIVE
NATURE
by Carl B. Charles

THE VOICE OF VOICES

Nature is a breathtaking sight
Of vibrant colors and enchanting sounds
Trees swaying in the wind
Streams flowing peacefully around.
Flowers blooming in the summer heat
Leaves falling in autumn's hue
Birds singing their melodic beat
Butterflies fluttering in view.
Nature is a place of peace
A sanctuary for the mind
A momentary release
From the chaos of daily grind.
It reminds us that we are a part of something greater
Infinite and grand
And urges us to protect its heart
So that its beauty may forever stand.
Nature is a precious gift
One to cherish and preserve
For it is the source of life's lift
And allows our souls to swerve.

CHAPTER SIX
PERFECT PEACE
by Diane Fabien

THE VOICE OF VOICES

I want to be your peacekeeper
I want to make everything perfect when it comes between us
I want to make our relationship come into love full of passion.
You made my heart skip a thousand beats
I love the way you make me feel like I'm at peace
I'm glad we made it through together.
We are going to last forever
It feels like the love in my heart mimics the one in yours
I love the things we do together
And it makes me happy and healthy
You always keep me warm when I need you to
Here together is where I always want to stay
Because in my dreams and my heart you'll always stay
I will never leave your side. I'll always stick with you no matter what
And my love for you will always be valued

CHAPTER SEVEN
HER IMAGINATION
by Estherlande Vigile

THE VOICE OF VOICES

She imagined this road she was walking on
It was a hot rainy day; she walked in the rain without hesitating,
Without any thoughts, she asked herself "Oh, why?"
"Why am I walking like this in the rain,
why is it painfully comforting?"
She started walking slower and slower,
within each droplet came a tear, perhaps a tear of joy....
Maybe even a tear of sadness.
Moments after, she stopped walking,
slowly sat down in the rain came a second.
She lay down with her wings opened.
She laid there staring into space, lost in her thoughts.
Came a thought of being dead!
She had deep thoughts, extremely deep thoughts
After a few minutes, she gets up and called the tears to leave and come back when necessary....
Came a moment of joy to a moment of sadness......
The end

CHAPTER EIGHT
THERE'S THIS PERSON
by Kinberlie Joseph

THE VOICE OF VOICES

There's this person,
-Someone who came from a witchcraft family.
-Someone who sees ghost.
-Someone who couldn't talk but has a lot to say.

-Someone who's scared of their own heart.
-Someone who's get lost in their own thoughts.
-Someone who's emotionally weak.
-Someone who locks herself in the restroom to end the pain.

-Someone who smokes with strangers.
-Someone who lost themselves in drugs, alcohol, and relationship.
-Someone who suffers from anxiety, depression, and witchcraft.
-Someone who sneak out at night to find pleasure.
-Someone who's scared to fall asleep at night.

There's this person,
-Someone who's able to move forward.
-Someone who is a fighter.
-Someone who got delivered from evil Spirits.
-Someone who was dead and reborn again.
-Someone whose heart is clean.
-Someone who knows the meaning of life in God.
-Someone who received the Holy Spirit on January 1, 2023.
-Someone who's going to heaven.
-Someone who is saved and represent herself as a woman of God.
And that person is me, Kinberlie Joseph.

CHAPTER NINE
RESPECTING OTHERS
by Alley Bazile

THE VOICE OF VOICES

Respecting others is just the beginning, it entails more than simply listening with your heart. Showing kindness, being fair, and making sure everyone is aware.

Respecting each other, regardless of the day, it is critical to pay attention to what they say. Giving space and understanding with grace is a way of demonstrating the humanity of our species.

Why is respect important? Without respect, the world would be in chaos, with dictatorships ruling instead of the diplomacy we all seek. Impatience and one-sided arguments would reign. Low self-esteem and depression would become more prevalent.

Respecting each other and being able to cooperate with respectable differences is the only way we can all come out true. Compassion and kindness are what make a person wise. Not only in friendships but also at work and school. Respecting each other's opinions and voices is the best way to make the right decision.

CHAPTER TEN
HEALED ME
by Venissa Louissaint

THE VOICE OF VOICES

I wish I knew the thought I had about you
I can't always articulate the way I feel
I wish I could explain the feeling you gave me
When I wake up to your face.
The way my heart jumps for you
When you say my name
I wish I knew how to describe It to a stranger

The song that reminds me of you
Your smell that lingers
Around my thought
It surprises me of how you healed me
In ways I didn't know

Where possibly you were perfectly
Craft cell by cell
Sunlight infused into your veins
Like a precious angel
So why do tears fall
When you are made of star

CHAPTER ELEVEN
SELF WORTH AND SELF-LOVE
by Gardina Jean-Baptiste

THE VOICE OF VOICES

Loving yourself is tough.
Waking up every day with a proud sense of who you are can feel exhausting, or even impossible.
But we all know, deep down, we can be the best versions of ourselves when we love ourselves fiercely and freely.
Sometimes it takes mantras and prayers and sticky notes on the wall and chats in the mirror to make self-love stick.

Self-love poems to remind you of your worth and value in this world; to bring you to a centered place of peace within yourself.

Self-love is a revolution that every atom in your body is marching for.

You are not small.
You are not unworthy.
You are not insignificant.

The universe wove you from a constellation, just so atom,
every fire in you comes from a different star.

Together, you are bound by stardust, altogether spectacular created by the energy of the universe itself.

And that, my darling, is the poetry of physics, the poetry of you.

Accept yourself as work in progress to continue

To build yourself into the person you're dreaming to be.

The person you potentially could be.

Accept your flaws, accept your truths.

Accept your past.

And make light of them; no one can tear you down if you make peace with who you are and where you've been.

If you are going to focus on the negativity, focus on turning them into positivity.

Focus on growing.

Often, our minds is the scariest place to be.

It'll trick you into comparing yourself to others and it'll trick you into believing you aren't good enough...But you are.
You have always been, and you always will be.

You're much more powerful when you believe in yourself.

If you don't love all of you, who will??

THE VOICE OF VOICES

CHAPTER TWELVE
HIGH
by Ciarra Morestan

THE VOICE OF VOICES

The moment of life
Where we're free
Even for a second,
That split second
Where the feeling
Is a black hole
Winter wonderland
With own beast
We try to slave the demons
But nothing just defeats
Is this what you want
Check mate you WON
High will only be an understatement
They cry at night that's the statement
What's not to understand
We drown in thoughts
That was once fought
Their own battles weren't happy
Like our thoughts are an elf on a self
Feeling disowned can't see their self
when all they want is for someone to listen
For that help, to pay attention
Can't live in these four dimensions
I guess HIGH is the conclusion
For their dimension

CHAPTER THIRTEEN
THUNDERSTORM
by Sara Juste

THE VOICE OF VOICES

Who am I? What am I capable of?

I am a small birch hanging on to the ground
    tightly trying not to get blown
I am a tiny Meerkat trying not to get seduced by a puff adder.
I am a blind and deaf woman crossing the street without any guidance.
I always try not to let my imaginations rein
because I know what I am capable of
Sometimes I think of things that shouldn't come across my mind
But by the grace of God, I will never accomplish those ideas.

CHAPTER FOURTEEN
DARK SKIN GIRLS
by Marlande Alliance Maëlle

THE VOICE OF VOICES

Dark skin girls
Skin just like pearl
The best thing in the world
Far from freedom
When we came from the bottom

Dark skin girls
Your skin is a reminder of everything
A tragic past you went in
Sweet, lucid, and brown
Warm desire is her crown

Dark skin girls
We see you; we hear you
We fight for you, we champion you
Why don't they just embrace
That everybody has got a grace

Dark skin girls
You walk into a room
Just as cool as you please
Into a man the fellows stand, or fall on their knees
Phenomenally
Phenomenal woman

Dark skin girls
The music you listen to
Even the hair you have too

But always remember no one
Ever can come close to being like you

Dark skin girls
Your skin just like pearls
The best thing in the world
I'll never trade you for anybody else
Dark skin girls, black is beautiful.

THE VOICE OF VOICES

CHAPTER FIFTEEN
TRUTH
by Thed-Fana Prince

THE VOICE OF VOICES

I am a ten but don't see that,
when I get complimented it's hard to believe and just say AMEN
I deal with difficulties that goes unnoticed and untold,
putting on an act of positivity and moving on
Whether there's light or darkness each day, every hour,
every minute and second…they're all the same
Just get up, smile, hurting or not <u>ACT</u> normal
We all know and see each and every single one of us
but not each other's pain nor glories
not even OK moments, let alone bad moments
We can show and prove that we don't care
but then we're the bad guy
so we're living up to PARENTS', FRIENDS' PARTNERS'
expectations but not our own
One mistake you get disowned and chase away with them asking
no explanation whatsoever
You do and give but not appreciated or seen
Borrow you are suddenly a thief
Get made fun of it's okay in the others' point of view,
FINALLY react… you turn out wrong
Cannot give up and won't that's just IT
That's just LIFE

CHAPTER SIXTEEN
I AM
by Gally Ducasse

THE VOICE OF VOICES

I am respectful and honest
I wonder about my future
I hear a bell ringing
I see my future
I want to travel the world
I am respectful and honest
I pretend I am an actress
I feel an invisible friend
I touch the stars
I worried about myself and others
I cry about losing a loved one
I am respectful and honest
I understand life
I say there is a way
I dream about me flying
I try hard to get something I want
I hope all my dream are come true
I am respectful and honest

CHAPTER SEVENTEEN
I AM
by Ketnaydine Edouard

THE VOICE OF VOICES

I am brave and honest.
I wonder how many people suffering.
I hear Angel's voice.
I see the heaven's gate opening.
I want to do it all over again.
I am brave and honest.
I pretend I am a invisible.
I feel like a rock.
I touch the sky.
I worry about dying.
I cry for my country.
I am brave and honest.
I understand how the society is.
I say education is the key.
I dream of becoming a doctor.
I try my best to understand people's emotions.
I hope to stop worrying about others and put myself first.
I am brave and honest.

CHAPTER EIGHTEEN
BEAUTY
by Sanaa Robertson

THE VOICE OF VOICES

Roses are red,
Violets are blue,
Your song is merry,
And so are you.
Orchids are white,
Ghost ones are rare,
An appearance is wavy,
And so is your hair.
Magnolia grows,
With buds like eggs,
A run is short,
And so are your legs.
Sunflowers reach,
Up to the skies,
A sunlight is dazzling,
And so are your eyes.
Foxgloves in hedges,
Surround the farms,
The side is safe,
And so are your arms.
Daisies are pretty,
Daffies have style,
Purposes are illuminating,
And so is your smile.
A butterfly is beautiful,
Just like you.

CHAPTER NINETEEN
TRUE WARRIOR
by Richard Paul

THE VOICE OF VOICES

I bet you don't know how it feels
To make it to the top after having everyone around you thinking you're going to flop.
I bet you don't know how it feels to have those close to you talking about you,
They talk about you behind your back,
real talk it hurts and that's a fact.
I bet you don't know how it feels, to give someone the world but instead your heart ripped out your chest and stomped on the floor...
after you know damn well you did your best.

You see, what I realize is people going to hate on your glory,
without even knowing your story.
They judge you blindly, take you lightly, assume you aren't mighty, and act confused when they see you react wisely. But regardless of what people say, I'm going to take control of my destiny and show them the best of me, despite the amount of pain my chest can beat, I'll always work my way up no need to cheat.

Man, I never had no handouts, But I made sure I'd be the main person to stand out.
I've been through hell and back, they didn't expect me to do so well because I'm black but I continue to surprise them, I mean I look like nothing where I came from...empty plates, upset face, honestly, I could've used a happy place but I use my past as propane and I'll share my story on this stage with no shame.

My point is don't stress how you start, because if you continue to do you, success and hard work will set you apart. My name is Richard Paul a mountain climber, but you might as well call me a True Warrior.

CHAPTER TWENTY
DREAMS
by Axel Gomez-Montepeq

THE VOICE OF VOICES

I thirst to cross the darkness.
And finally, to be able to cover your waist like a dream. Where I managed to cover my origin, like the tears of a child who longs to return to his mother again.

I maintain the torture of the hunger of an old being,
which subjects me to the abyss of darkness.
The cry of pleasure when the rain falls envelops my being.
Fresh breeze that fills me with memories of yesterday.
A whole compass to regret having abandoned you.
My dear maiden.

Unnamed feelings must possess me.
I must appreciate our now and hate the past.
Olive leaves grow and perish over time,
I cry without regret for the now and the never.

Fantasy was the remaining constant in the equation that occasionally clouded my judgment. And the missing formula is gone.

CHAPTER TWENTY-ONE
LOVE
by Ketnaydine Edward

THE VOICE OF VOICES

Love, the best thing ever
Love, a feeling that lasts forever
Love, the laughter you brought me
If my heart could speak, I would tell you
How much I adore you
Hard to approach, easy to fall for
The feelings are bursting out
Wants to go for something brand-new
Must let the feelings break-through.
Love, the best thing ever
A love that'll last forever
No matter the problem
I'll put you on top, it's no deal
I'll be the bottom
I stay falling for your smile
I get up but it's like you pushed my heart to keep falling.
Your laughter brighter than the sun
With your voice being soft like a ball of cotton
You threw me, and I just flew
Your love bringing me higher
You not knowing any better
Making me fall for you forever

CHAPTER TWENTY-TWO
7 BILLION PATHS
by Medefca Metellus

THE VOICE OF VOICES

7 billion paths but you choose mine
Long, but you keep walking
Another path came for you and
you still walk on my path
Even if I put cactus to hurt you
You still walk on it
7 billion paths, but you choose my dark one
Every step you take
You add a light
You never give up on my path
No matter what happen
You still walk waiting for the end.

CHAPTER TWENTY-THREE
LIFE
by Gally Ducasse

THE VOICE OF VOICES

Life gets harder everyday
No time to think, no time to play
When will this madness cease?
Where is free time? Where is peace?
I've been in misery
Lost on a journey
Although the sun is bright
I can't see no light
Life is like a dream
Life gets hot like a steam
Life is unimaginable
But it's not going to always be stable
With all things impossible
Comes the irresistible
The rhyme of life I give to you
You'll find it true

CHAPTER TWENTY-FOUR
WOMEN EMPOWERMENT
by Marlina Souffrantt

THE VOICE OF VOICES

The world laughs
When she cries,
It ignores her
When she tries something nice.

I am confident,
I remove doubt, I stand with the truth,
I build my own faith...

We come away
With our head held high
And an elegance
That cannot be denied.

Women of yesterday and today,
We share responsibilities in the society
For the greater good of humanity,
Rise up, beat the odds, demonstrate unity in diversity.

Warriors Blood they bleed
Their sole purpose is to help us in need
Helping us to succeed
Women are the real warriors indeed

CHAPTER TWENTY-FIVE
WHO AM I
by Meilleur Florelea

THE VOICE OF VOICES

Someone who is patient and care
Someone who believes in me
Someone who always pushes to do better
Someone who is confident
Someone who never stop thinking where the future will take her
Someone who knows where she comes from and know where she is going
Someone who stratified herself about what she got
Someone who is confident
Someone who never give up on herself

Dr. Judith Grey's Poetry Club of 2022/2023

CHAPTER TWENTY-SIX
WHERE I'M FROM
by Aliya Baptiste

THE VOICE OF VOICES

The beaches are as blue as the sky
Where flamingos roam around the land
Where kids run behind ice cream trucks

Where elders will always hound.
The atmosphere over there is timeless
Laughs you have on late nights outside is worth more than gold
Nieces and cousins by the beach we were mindless

Where I'm from is filled with reggae, soccer, rake, and scrape
Where I'm from we are proud to rock our black gold and aqua
which can be seen above the landmarks and under sea

Where tourist enjoy vacation
Where the smell of grilled conch fills the air
Where coconut trees are our main worry
Yes, I am proud to say i am Bahamian

CHAPTER TWENTY-SEVEN
NEEDS OF THE WORLD
by Daniel Gonzalez

THE VOICE OF VOICES

The world is very beautiful with all its flaws,
Although something makes this world very disturbing,
They do not know how to forgive or how to grow,
False promise that politicians makes when speaking,
It is as if values and studies were low,
And everybody knows
Simply nobody wants to say it
Because in every mind have fear to be down
But with these words we are going to break it,
And we are going to know who is at fault.

But first, we need to know what the world needs
And like this we will know how can we change that.
It's too obvious to see that we don't have love here
And we know that 'cause when somebody needs a hand
Ain't nobody want to help, they just focus on laughing,
It's too easy to laugh or criticize
Criticism of anyone who asks for rights
They judge the one who helps those who nobody help
They annoy all those who get tired of injustices
It's too easy to make fun of them
Make injustice for everyone that just want to be safe,
But it's difficult for them to help and turn their backs on popular opinion
They just want power and want to have the people dancing and laughing
But they don't want that the people to know what is true
They don't want others to see the beautiful blue sky
They don't want people to be happy and fly.

Actually, we can see that the problem start in our house
They no longer teach values and never see reality
And in every injustice, our family just say: just because.
Is that's the world that we want to live in?
Is that's the world that we want for the next generations?
We can't live like this anymore
And now we know who is to be blamed
Who is the liar
When and where the problem starts.

It's too beautiful this world, with the environment,
With the animals and what we see outside the planet
But it's not beautiful what we have in our hearts
We need to be happy, we need freedom,
We need to help everyone that need help
We need love
In conclusion, that's the needs of the world.

THE VOICE OF VOICES

CHAPTER TWENTY-EIGHT
FAMILY KINDNESS AND LOVE
by Frederick Hyppolite

THE VOICE OF VOICES

I always see the feeling and care that is around in my life
My family members can help one another with togetherness
One father is working to get money for a better cause
One mother is much loving and caring
My mother is still what she is to care for my family in needs
she been cooking meals like rice, chicken, and pasta,
cleaning around in the house every week
and took care of her grandkids as well
She has been working at the same job
for more than a decade longer
giving advice about being responsible and doing well to me,
my brothers, and my sister
My mom will always be loving to her family.
One brother is always helpful around the house
One sister takes care of her two young sons
and one young daughter
Those two words are making my family feel proud
and better at doing the right way
God has helped this family from their sad and uncaring moments
My family will keep on helping and teaching each other to being
kindness and love to this year of 2023.

CHAPTER TWENTY-NINE
YOUR LOVE
by Emely Acosta

THE VOICE OF VOICES

Your love is like a sweet summer breeze
Blowing through my heart with ease
The warmth of your embrace
Fills me with your grace
I'm grateful for the love you bring to me

Lighting up my life seem divine
Your beautiful smile and heart of gold
Make me feel so young and bold
I'm blessed to have you in my life

Your thoughtfulness fills me with joy
Your compassion brings me peace and calm
Your understanding nature soothes my soul
And your friendship makes me feel whole
You truly are a special kind of love

Your love is eternal and pure
It fills me with joy
And I'm sure that I will love you forever
For you my heart will never sever
Your love is the most beautiful thing in my life

CHAPTER THIRTY
BARON DOCTOR
by Christ Thomas

THE VOICE OF VOICES

A smell of blood and corpse remains among the sugarcane;
it is a pervasive, nauseating scent.

The graves are crammed with damaged bones
and wordless death-rattles amongst the coconut trees.
The fragile tyrant is speaking while wearing a top hat, owl glasses,
and a large stomach.

The quick chuckles with gloves on and the three crown palace
shines like a watch.

At times, enter the hallways and join the blue mouths
and dead voices that have just been buried.
The crying is invisible, like a plant whose seeds perpetually fall to
the ground and whose big,
blind leaves sprout even in the absence of light.
It's time to stop licking our wounds.
Utilizing kneeling and earth-digging techniques.

We need to meet up once right now before moving forward:
One is joined hands at the end of the night! Cut off your head
Burn your house Make One pile of your hate One big pile of
their tenets Bring tar, pine tree Lamp oil, and let it all burn Stop
sleeping to guide our actions! Anger grew to scale, blow after blow,
swamp in terrible water, muzzle full of pus and silence Where!
Where to shame you, Doc In the desert city, in the dust of the
cathedral, In the forgotten, in the mountain ports, or on their rise?

CHAPTER THIRTY-ONE
I AM ALIYA
by Aliya Baptiste

THE VOICE OF VOICES

A girl that uses to skips school
A girl that you to want to die
A girl that tried to commit suicide
A girl that felt like she had no one
A girl that cries herself to sleep
A girl that uses to cut herself
A girl that was depressed
A girl that use to smoke
A girl that use to vape
A girl that was in the wrong crowd
A girl that didn't fully believe in God
A girl that was invited to dance and didn't know her life was going to change
A girl that started to go to church more
A girl that got baptized
A girl that got the Holy Spirit
A girl that's not alone anymore
A girl that got a church family
A girl that is proud to say she came a long way
A girl that now has a future
A girl that is on a Journey with God
A girl that is proud to say she's a Christian
A girl that never knew where she was going
but know where she came from and know exactly where she is going now
Yes, I am that girl I am Aliya

CHAPTER THIRTY-TWO
MY FLYING ANGEL
by Moresha Guillaume

THE VOICE OF VOICES

Feeling like your world is crashing down right in front of you
Feeling numb like you have no power over what's happening
So, you start begging God to make a miracle happen
Then someone comes in your life changing your entire life
Feeling like you're in heaven
Praying for this to never end.

It's like God send me a flying angel to save me
But nothing last forever like they all say
One day my flying angel fly away saying to wait for him
Not a second have gone by without thinking about him
I feel like a part of me went missing
Having flashback of the good memories

Hearing the voice playing over and over
Playing inside my head like a favorite song
I feel like everyone is moving on
But I am stuck in the same place
Waiting till he come flying back to me.

CHAPTER THIRTY-THREE
LIFE WITHOUT MOTHER
by Patrianna Reyna Astin

THE VOICE OF VOICES

You brought me for nine months with a lot of suffering, pain, and vomiting
Life without you mommy is like taking a bullet through my heart
Getting up in the morning without you and not with the warmth of your body
It hurts my little heart to know that you're in this world
But I can't feel your heart against my heart

At my school when I watch the children with their mothers
Or hear them talk about theirs
I wonder how you are
If I could do something to get you back home
I would but I can't

In the morning, noon and at nights I think of you
At night I overflow with tears thinking of you
My heart is collapsing my brain has and had enough
Life will never be the same without you.

CHAPTER THIRTY-FOUR
MY DAY
by Olivier Cotiere

THE VOICE OF VOICES

The day came
I woke up
I stretched
I pottered
I nibbled
I dreamed
I wondered
I kissed
I loved

The day went and I have done nothing, yet I have done everything.

CHAPTER THIRTY-FIVE
OPEN WATERS
by Elijah Joseph

THE VOICE OF VOICES

I AM THE SEA THAT HOLDS LIFE.
I AM THE THING PEOPLE FIND NICE BUT ALSO FIND A PUZZLE.
I AM THE THING THAT HOLD BOTH THE DARKNESS AND THE LIGHT.
I AM THE SEA THAT ALLOWS LIVING THINGS TO GROW.
I AM THE ONE WHO CAN'T BE STOP NO MATTER WHAT COMES MY WAY.
I AM WHAT KEEPS THE WORLD ALIVE
I AM THE ONE WHO ALLOWS COLORS TO COME TO LIFE
I AM THE ONE WHO IS EVERYWHERE
I AM THE ONE WHO PEOPLE SEE AS FUN AND SAD
I AM THE SEA.

CHAPTER THIRTY-SIX
DELUSIONAL POEM
by Nachca Pierre

THE VOICE OF VOICES

Beautifully seen, though senselessly rather than being helpful
All the pointless imaginations
Blocking all the illusions rather than believing the reality
We trust in the anxiety but there was no solution,
I could not find any, yet I knew there were so many delivered in the world
Forgetting every word, unimaginably surreal,
Can't even believe I'm living for real,
The love of the world leaving in the past
The world fades believing it would always be fast rather than it being delayed.

CHAPTER THIRTY-SEVEN
JOURNEY TO HOME
by Unika Pierre

THE VOICE OF VOICES

Living in an unknown world

Lost and unwanted

Struggling to make it alive.

Oh, I wonder how life is in Heaven

I pretend to be okay

But those silent cries kill at nights

Imprison with past mistakes

Will I make it, Home?

But I hear God saying: "Come back home daughter

Because you are forgiven and love by Me."

Oh, How I love you, My Lord.

Flying in the sky to Heaven

I am accepted and loved by Jesus Christ

CHAPTER THIRTY-EIGHT
LIKE A PHOENIX I RISE FROM THE ASHES
by Kaytora Paul

THE VOICE OF VOICES

No matter the amount of pain
No matter the amount of tears
No matter the amount of lashes
Like phoenix I rise from the ashes

My heart may ache
My eyes may swell
My body may be riddled with gashes, but
Like a phoenix I rise from the ashes

Even if I'm dejected
Even if I'm in deep somber
Even when it all crashes
Like a phoenix I rise from the ashes

CHAPTER THIRTY-NINE
THE PLAYBOY
by Charvens Sainteus

THE VOICE OF VOICES

How apathetic will you get

A destroyer, a devil, a monster

Anything you set your eyes on get damaged

Not once you tried to be conscientious

Now look at you

Would be funny if it wasn't so sad

Been hypnotized by pleasure

Now pleasure becomes pain

You're trying to change now!

So many opportunities

Yet none were taken

Now it's too late

Went from the predator to the prey

The things that a victim can do

Now you cannot stop bleeding

And the last breath was taken

CHAPTER FORTY
VARIATIONS ON DREAMS
by Ferlens Frederic

THE VOICE OF VOICES

To open wide my arms
Till the white day is over, to spin and dance.
Then take a nap in a sunny area on a chilly evening.

In the lull nightfall,
Beneath a large tree
That is my idea to be black like me!

To open wide my arms
Dancing with the sun on my face!
Whirl, Whirl! Until the brief finished.

Relax in the drab evening
A large, skinny tree
Coming softly Black like me is in the night.

CHAPTER FORTY-ONE
A POEM TO MY MOM
by Leissa Puthiot

THE VOICE OF VOICES

To the woman who has always protected me.
I want you to know
How grateful I am
That you are my mother.

You held my hand throughout my life
And showed me not only
How to get through the hard times
But how to help others through them as well
You're an exceptional woman
So strong and so wise

You are the perfect role model for your children
I appreciate your good character
Your respect for others
Your willingness to lend a helping hand
Even if it's inconvenient for you.

I am so very grateful for your love
A motherly love
That's give me purpose and direction
As well as peaceful inner security.

Mommy, let me just say...
There are no words to express
How grateful I am
That you were born
And that God chose you
To be my mother

                Your Loving daughter

CHAPTER FORTY-TWO
I ONCE SAID
by Carla Louis

THE VOICE OF VOICES

Karma always comes back at you!

I once said, "I hope you break an ankle."

I once said, "I hate this life all because of you."

I once said, "Good luck, break a leg."

I once said, "He/she's doing this for attention."

I once said, "Damn, all that she's getting, where's mine."

I once said, "Wow, I really want this."

I once said, "All this you're doing is too much."

I once realize all of those are karma.

Karma hits me, good and bad.

I once learned to never judge.

I once learned to be nicer and much kinder.

I once said and felt.

I once said and regret.

I once said and realized.

I once said and learn.

I once said, said and said enough.

CHAPTER FORTY-THREE
FREE
by Dennis Brown-Figueroa

THE VOICE OF VOICES

Weightless in the ocean, I float free,
My troubles fade away, and with them, the world's debris.
In the art of swimming, I find my peace.

Each stroke represents an unbroken chain.
I am free from the bonds that bound me,
Free from the weight of life,
And free from the sufferings that previously defined me.

With each breath, I inhale new optimism and release everything that drags me down.
The water transforms into a canvas on which I paint my aspirations and passion.
As I glide and soar through the liquid blue
The rhythm of my heart beats in harmony with the calm ebb and flow of the water.
I am at once free and whole, as I am reborn.

So let me swim forevermore,
And find the freedom that my heart longs for.
In the art of swimming, I'll find my way,
And be free to live, love, and play.

CHAPTER FORTY-FOUR
LOVE
by Barbara Auguste

THE VOICE OF VOICES

Love can be good
Love can be bad
Love can be happy
Love can be sad
We find love in the depths of our hearts
Where some secrets are hidden
Where no one can know and see
Where the river embraces the sea
Where the moon and water meet
Where Romeo and Juliet meet
And two
Souls connect
Butterflies fly away
This is the end of our beginning

CHAPTER FORTY-FIVE
HAPPINESS
by Curtis Dorcely

THE VOICE OF VOICES

What is happiness?
Is it just a finesse?
A drug that gives you a nest,
And keep you away from your pest.

A drug that gives you a pause,
From which you cannot overdose.
Comes with no cost,
Beautiful like a frost

Temporally make life better,
Even thought life might get harder.
Happiness is being home again
Happiness is walking with no pain

Happiness is family to me
Happiness in the faces, I longed to see
Happiness is once more being free
Happiness that grows like a tree

CHAPTER FORTY-SIX
LOVE'S BEAUTY POEM
by Dorothy Lodz-Chamma Pierre

THE VOICE OF VOICES

Love is a flame that burns so bright,
It warms the soul on coldest night.
It starts with just a tiny spark,
And grows until it fills the heart.
Love is a song that fills the air,
It whispers secrets, sweet and rare.
It echoes through the mountaintops,
And dances with the ocean's drops.
Love is a flower that blooms with care,
It blossoms in the summer air.
It fills the world with colors bright,
And spreads its fragrance day and night.
Love is a journey we all must take,
It leads us through each bend and break.
It's full of twists and turns and bends,
But with each step, our love ascends.
Love is a gift we all should cherish,
It's something we should never perish.
It's what connects us all as one,
And makes this life worth living on.

CHAPTER FORTY-SEVEN
ABROAD
by Unika Pierre

THE VOICE OF VOICES

My Love!

Oh, how lovely she is

Unfathomable love

More valuable than rubies

Even if life was difficult, she consistently made me joyful.

Every encounter with her was transformative.

Time was slipping away as the clock continued to tick.

Even though she was moving, she was unaware of the date.

Her time was cherished.

My Love, Why

How could you abandon me?

How should I proceed now that you are gone?

Time was short

Did not have time to express my love more

But you were aware

How much I appreciate you, My Love

All thanks given to the efforts of
Dr. Judith Grey.

An outstanding educator,
who nurtures students' creativity.

Judith E. Grey has over 30 years of teaching experience in both the Caribbean and the United States of America. She is an expert in Adult Education and is currently an educator at North Miami Adult Education Center. Dr. Grey earned a Doctor of Education (Ed. D) in Educational Leadership, Master of Science (MS) in Educational Administration, and Graduate Certificate in Educational Administration from St. Thomas University in Miami Gardens, Florida. Dr. Grey also holds a Master of Science (MS) in TESOL from the University of Miami in Florida.

She is certified in the Florida Public School system and holds National Boards' Certification and Florida Leadership certifications. Her areas of research interest and expertise include school administration, multiculturalism, and parental involvement as well as technology integration in education. She is currently the president for The National Board-Certified Teachers of Miami Dade Inc. Dr. Grey is an effective communicator, a pillar of her community, a problem solver, and a strategic thinker.

www.ingramcontent.com/pod-product-compliance
Lightning Source LLC
Chambersburg PA
CBHW052109110526
44592CB00013B/1536